MW00574473

SOLO SOUNDS

FOR TUBA

Piano Accompaniment-Levels 3-5　　　　　　**Volume 1**

Cover Credit: Ace Music Center, North Miami, Florida
Yamaha International Corporation Musical Instrument Division

Editor: Jack Lamb

© 1987 Belwin Mills Publishing Corp. (ASCAP)
All Rights Assigned to and Controlled by Alfred Publishing Co., Inc.
All Rights Reserved including Public Performance. Printed in USA.

EL03354

Changing Scene

Richard W. Bowles

© 1973 (Renewed 2001) Belwin Mills Publishing Corp. (ASCAP)
All Rights Assigned to and Controlled by Alfred Publishing Co., Inc.
All Rights Reserved including Public Performance. Printed in USA.

Sonata No. 7
(1st Movement)

Franz Joseph Haydn
Arranged by Richard W. Bowles

© 1973 (Renewed 2001) Belwin Mills Publishing Corp. (ASCAP)
All Rights Assigned to and Controlled by Alfred Publishing Co., Inc.
All Rights Reserved including Public Performance. Printed in USA.

(Theme Group II)

In The Hall Of The Mountain King

E. Grieg
Arranged by Fred Weber

© 1973 (Renewed 2001) Belwin Mills Publishing Corp. (ASCAP)
All Rights Assigned to and Controlled by Alfred Publishing Co., Inc.
All Rights Reserved including Public Performance. Printed in USA.

Largo And Presto

Benedetto Marcello
Arranged by Donald C. Little
Figured bass realization by
George R. Belden

© 1978 (Renewed 2006) Belwin Mills Publishing Corp. (ASCAP)
All Rights Assigned to and Controlled by Alfred Publishing Co., Inc.
All Rights Reserved including Public Performance. Printed in USA.

Allegro
(from Sonata No. 3)

Antonio Vivaldi
Arranged by Ken Swanson

© 1971 (Renewed 1999) Belwin Mills Publishing Corp. (ASCAP)
All Rights Assigned to and Controlled by Alfred Publishing Co., Inc.
All Rights Reserved including Public Performance. Printed in USA.

Menuetto

W.A. Mozart
Arranged by Ken Swanson

© 1971 (Renewed 1999) Belwin Mills Publishing Corp. (ASCAP)
All Rights Assigned to and Controlled by Alfred Publishing Co., Inc.
All Rights Reserved including Public Performance. Printed in USA.

23

24

Slumber Song

A. Gretchaninoff
Arranged by Ken Swanson

© 1971 (Renewed 1999) Belwin Mills Publishing Corp. (ASCAP)
All Rights Assigned to and Controlled by Alfred Publishing Co., Inc.
All Rights Reserved including Public Performance. Printed in USA.

26

Honor And Arms

G. Handel
Arranged by William Bell

© 1965 by **FIRST DIVISION PUBLISHING CORPORATION**
© Assigned to **BELWIN MILLS PUBLISHING CORP. (ASCAP)**
All Rights Assigned to and Controlled by Alfred Publishing Co., Inc.
All Rights Reserved including Public Performance. Printed in USA.

Carmen Excerpts

Georges Bizet
Arranged by William Bell

© 1965 by FIRST DIVISION PUBLISHING CORPORATION
© Assigned to Belwin Mills Publishing Corp. (ASCAP)
All Rights Assigned to and Controlled by Alfred Publishing Co., Inc.
All Rights Reserved including Public Performance. Printed in USA.

His Majesty The Tuba

Robert Dowling

Introduction

© 1940 (Renewed 1964) Belwin Mills Publishing Corp. (ASCAP)
All Rights Assigned to and Controlled by Alfred Publishing Co., Inc.
All Rights Reserved including Public Performance. Printed in USA.

40